PRINCE LANCE GOES TO THE DENTIST

Written by Madison Symonne
Illustrated by Lana Lee
Edited by Katrina Sprague

Dedicated To:

Our father who believes in our dreams.

We love you, Daddy!

ISBN-13 979-8-218-18375-2

Take a trip with Prince Lance to the dentist.

What new things will he learn?

KIDS DENTAL OFF

"OUCH! Mommy, Mommy!" cried Prince Lance.

"Yes, baby, what's wrong?" Mommy asked.

"My tooth hurts!"
he groaned.

"Open wide," said Daddy

"Ahhhh - OUCH!" Prince Lance cried as he opened his mouth.

"Prince Lance, did you eat that lollipop last night?" asked Daddy.

Prince Lance put his head down slowly and said, "Yes, Daddy."

"Prince Lance, didn't Mommy and Daddy tell you not to eat the lollipop?" asked Daddy.

"Yes, but it looked SO good. Ouch..." Prince Lance said while holding his mouth.

"Well Prince Lance, when Mommy and I tell you not do something, you should listen. Our job is to protect you and your beautiful smile," said Daddy.

"Now we need to take you to the dentist so you can feel better!"

"I feel better now Daddy. It does not – ow – hurt anymore," Lance said with a slight frown on his face.

"I know you do not like the dentist, baby, but Dr. Mela is great. She will take good care of you!" Mommy said.

While in the car, Mommy and Daddy started to sing as Prince Lance looked out the window trying to think of a way out of going to the dentist.

♪♪ Where are we going? D-E-N-T-I-S-T ♪♪

🎶 **D** is for Disneyland - Prince Lance is going soon 🎶

🎶 **E** is for Eating - Prince Lance's favorite food 🎶

🎶 **N** is for Nice - Dr. Mela gives good advice 🎶

🎶 **T** is for Tent - for an outdoor camping event 🎶

🎶 **I** is for Island - Prince Lance's playground out of town 🎶

🎶 **S** is for Sunshine - Prince Lance will always be mine 🎶

🎶 **T** is for Tickling - while we laugh and play 🎶

Prince Lance laughed at the original song made by his parents, and he forgot that he was going to the dentist!

"Look, Prince Lance, we are here," said Daddy.

Prince Lance looked at the building and hid his face behind his stuffed teddy bear.

"Good morning, Mr. and Mrs. Gold," said the dentist.

"Good morning, Dr. Mela," Mommy and Daddy responded.

"Good morning, Prince Lance. You look handsome today, and who do you have with you?" asked Dr. Mela.

"Good morning, Dr. Mela," Prince Lance said in a soft tone, "I have Prince Bear with me."

"Let me have Carla to take you back to my chair so that I can help you feel better," said Dr. Mela.

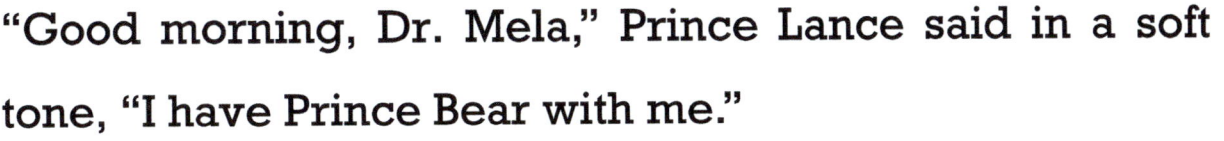

"Ok, Prince Lance, what is bothering you?"

"My tooth hurts really bad."

"Which one?"

Prince Lance pointed to his bottom left tooth.

"Aw, can you tell me what happened?" asked Dr. Mela.

"I was eating a lollipop, and when I bit the candy, my tooth started hurting," Lance told the dentist.

"Oh, I see. While candy may taste good, it's not the best choice for your teeth," said Dr. Mela.

"We will teach you how to choose healthy snacks after we get your tooth better."

"Now let's get started."

Dr. Mela pulled out her wand and worked her magic in Prince Lance's mouth, and in no time, he was feeling much better.

"Carla, will you bring my health snacks cart in?" asked Dr. Mela.

"Yes, Dr. Mela," said Carla.

"What can I have?"
Prince Lance asked excitedly.

"Well, what do you like to eat?" Dr. Mela asked.

"I like fruit," said Prince Lance smiling.

Dr. Mela smiled and said
"Well, here's some examples of
things you can eat."

- Apples
- Strawberries
- Carrots
- Cheese
- Pears
- Celery

"Now that you know of a few healthy snacks, let's go over how to floss your teeth," said Dr. Mela.

Floss at least once a day to help remove healthy food and snacks from between your teeth.

"Now that you know how to floss, I want you to brush at least twice a day for two minutes," instructed Dr. Mela.

Turn on your favorite song and brush to the beat!

"Next, I want you to rinse your mouth to remove the toothpaste."

"Finally, I want you to come see me every six months for check-ups and cleanings, so that I can keep that smile of yours beautiful."

Prince Lance smiled and gave Dr. Mela a hug.

"Thank you, Dr. Mela. I feel better now."

"You are welcome, Prince Lance. I can't wait to see you again."

Dr. Mela handed Prince Lance a dentist goodie bag which included a baseball toothbrush, toothpaste, mouthwash, and a magical wand just like the one she used to make his tooth better.

Prince Lance Activity

Which foods are considered healthy snacks?

A. Carrots
B. Chocolate Cake
C. Apples

How long should you brush your teeth?

A. 5 minutes
B. 9 minutes
C. 2 minutes

How often should you see your dentist?

A. Every 2 months
B. Every 8 months
C. Every 6 months

Prince Lance To-Do
Grab a grown up and have fun!

Materials:
1 Sheet of paper
1 Clear sheet protector
Dry erase markers
Dry eraser

Instructions:

Draw a big tooth on your piece of paper and place it in the sheet protector. You can add a smiley face, a flower, or your favorite animal to your tooth if you'd like.

Use your dry erase markers to add your favorite snacks to your tooth.

Now begin brushing your tooth with the dry eraser to practice your brushing skills and clean your tooth.

We hope you have fun brushing your tooth as a family!